Bible Study

7 SESSIONS FOR SMALL GROUP
AND PERSONAL USE

G000065793

The
Second
Coming

Living in the Light
of Jesus' Return

WAVERLEY ABBEY
TRUST

Copyright © 2007 Waverley Abbey Trust.

Published 2007 by Waverley Abbey Trust, Waverley Abbey House, Waverley Lane, Farnham, Surrey GU9 8EP, UK. Waverley Abbey Trust is the trading name of CWR. Registered Charity No. 294387. Registered Limited Company No. 1990308.

Reprinted 2011, 2014, 2017, 2019, 2021, 2023.

All rights reserved. No part of this publication may be reproduced, stored in a retrieval system, or transmitted, in any form or by any means, electronic, mechanical, photocopying, recording or otherwise, without the prior permission in writing of Waverley Abbey Trust.

For list of National Distributors, visit waverleyabbeytrust.org/distributors

Unless otherwise indicated, all Scripture references are from the Holy Bible: New International Version (NIV), copyright © 1973, 1978, 1984 by the International Bible Society.

Concept development, editing, design and production by Waverley Abbey Trust.

Cover image: istockphoto.com

Printed in the UK.

Paperback ISBN: 978-1-85345-422-6

Ebook ISBN: 978-1-78951-488-9

Contents

About Cover to Cover

The *Cover to Cover* Bible Study Guides are a popular series helping individuals and groups to engage with the Bible and to dig deeper.

The first studies were produced in 2002 by Selwyn Hughes and now cover more than 80 different themes, characters and books of the Bible, and compiled by various writers and Bible teachers.

How to get the best from the studies

The *Cover to Cover* studies are designed to be either worked through individually or in a group. Whichever way you are using the study we encourage you to begin with prayer, asking God through His Holy Spirit to work in your life through these studies. Then trust that He will!

Do allow enough time for the questions and exercises, not rushing through but allocating time to focus on questions that raise specific challenges.

If you are studying as a group you may find our online resources useful. Here you will find some extra video content and copies of the daily guide to distribute to the members. Visit **wvly.org/c2ccv** to discover what is available.

In group discussions do make use of the leader's notes at the end of the study. Ensure that you give everyone in the group time to share and avoid allowing one person to dominate conversation.

Please feel free to adapt the material according to your group's needs. Trust that God is with you, leading you and helping each one of you draw closer to Him.

About the Authors

Written by Selwyn Hughes

Selwyn Hughes (1928-2006) was the founder and Life President of CWR and for over forty years was the author of the highly popular devotional *Every Day with Jesus*. His international ministry as a writer, Bible teacher, evangelist and counsellor spanned over fifty years. He travelled the world presenting a wide range of seminars on various aspects of the Christian life including marriage, relationships and personal development. His legacy continues with the work of Waverley Abbey Trust.

With contributions from Ian Sewter

Ian Sewter has co-authored a number of studies in the *Cover to Cover* series and has helped to develop the *Every Day with Jesus* Bible reading notes. His passion is that God's Word should become a living Word in people's lives.

Daily Guide and video content by Andy Peck

Andy Peck is a Christian communicator who writes books, broadcasts and teaches the Bible in a way that aims to be clear, practical and accessible. His work has included time as a Bible teacher in a pastoral role in three churches in the south of England; as a coach and mentor with university students; as a writer and editor for *Christianity* magazine; and has served as a Bible teacher and trainer at Waverley Abbey Trust, a charity that aims to help apply God's truth in everyday life and relationships.

Introduction

A few decades ago, any mention of the end of the age or the imminence of Christ's return was dismissed by most Christians as 'doomsday preaching'. But not any more. The questions that seem uppermost in believers' minds are these: Is the return of Jesus Christ imminent? Will Christ's coming take place in our time? Are we truly living in the last days? In an age that is growing darker and darker, the truth of Christ's return to this world is a ray of hope that shines like an ever-brightening beam. The world's leaders once talked about the idea that through technology, science and education, humankind would be able to work out its human dilemmas and establish an ideal society. No serious thinker believes that today. Some of the world's leaders, of course, live in hope that the countries of the world can be brought together to form a universal utopia. It is a pipe dream. True peace will only come to this world when Christ returns to rule and reign as King of kings and Lord of lords.

The last 100 years have demonstrated, as no other period in history, the futility of trying to organise life without God. People have tried on a massive scale to thrust God out of the universe He has made. W.E. Henley depicted the feelings of modern society when he wrote,

> It matters not how straight the gate,
> How charged with punishments the scroll,
> I am the master of my fate;
> I am the captain of my soul.

What vanity! The master of his fate and the captain of his soul! Because the men and women of this age found it hard to believe in God, they transferred their faith to humankind. 'Glory to humanity in the highest' is their creed. Walt Whitman said he loved cattle and all dumb animals because they did not kneel down and say their prayers! The years went by and this worship of human nature grew popular because it pandered to the egotism in people's hearts. It was nice to be told that there was no such thing as original sin, that the Golden Age was inevitable and that, by gradual steps, humankind would move unaided to perfection. This belief made redemption unnecessary, emptied the cross of meaning and made the Church a joke. And then came two world wars. The first one, they said, would be the war to end all wars. But then came the second, greater and more terrifying. Now here we are in the twenty-first century with the proliferation of weapons of mass destruction, and in danger of blowing our planet to pieces. For the first time in history we have the potential for global destruction.

Another concern is that conservationists tell us our natural resources are dwindling, and unless something dramatic takes place, demand will soon exceed supply. We are burning up the earth's oxygen at a faster rate than it can be replaced. A car, travelling a distance of just over 600 miles, uses as much oxygen as a person breathes in a whole year. A large jet burns up 50 tons of oxygen in a single Atlantic crossing. Stephen Travis, in his book *The Jesus Hope*, says:

> The United States produces only 60 per cent of the oxygen it consumes and if we go on polluting the oceans and thereby killing the oxygen-producing sea plants, we could reach the stage where there is no longer enough oxygen to support human life. Then man will be like a beast of prey who runs out of victims – and starves to death.[1]

---

1 Stephen Travis, *The Jesus Hope* (London: Word Books, 1974 and Leicester: Inter-Varsity Press, 1980).

And what of pollution? Who would think that an innocent thing like aerosol spray could rise into the atmosphere and be a threat to our survival? We have littered the earth with items like indestructible plastics, poisonous chemicals and many other things; little realising that, by so doing, we are threatening our very existence.

These points are not unfounded pessimism but gritty realism. Apart from the fact of Christ's personal return, there is no hope for the inhabitants of this tiny planet we call earth and it is impossible to live either effectively or happily without hope. Psychologists are unanimous in maintaining that no personality can be healthy unless there is within that personality a sense of true optimism or hope – 'an expectation based on reality, that whatever one's current state may be, the future holds brighter and better experiences'. Isn't it interesting that many writers, poets and lyricists reflect in their works a deep sense of melancholy and gloom? Take, for example, George Orwell's *1984*, or Aldous Huxley's *Brave New World*. Both young and old alike combine to reflect a pessimism concerning the future that in its way is eloquent and strangely moving. Most people, when faced with such gloom and uncertainty as I have described, reach out for a substitute. They try such things as occultism, transcendental meditation, drugs etc. But they are false hopes. They pick you up but they soon let you down. Everything outside of Jesus Christ is blind optimism. He, and only He, can supply the human personality with the power it needs to function effectively in an age that is falling apart at the seams. How thankful we Christians ought to be that in the midst of the world's dark and dismal problems, we have a hope for the future.

Basis of Belief in the Second Coming

Opening Exercise

In 1911, King George V said, 'The English Bible is the first of national treasures, and in its spiritual significance the most valuable thing that this world affords.' How do most people now view the Bible?

Bible Readings

- ▶ Daniel 7:13–14
- ▶ Isaiah 53:1–9
- ▶ John 20:30–31
- ▶ Acts 1:1–11
- ▶ 2 Timothy 3:10–17
- ▶ 2 Peter 1:16–21

Opening Our Eyes

Before we begin we must ask ourselves a piercing question: On what grounds do we base our belief that one day Jesus Christ is going to return to this world? Is it based on Christian myth and legend or is it based on something more authoritative? The answer is, of course, that we base this belief entirely on what God's Word, the Bible, teaches us about the subject. One in every 30 verses of Holy Scripture predicts our Saviour's return, and for every single mention of His first advent, there are eight allusions to His second advent. Some might object to this and say, 'But how do we know the Bible is true?' This question is becoming one of the battle cries of our generation. I am amazed at the number of evangelical believers who are adopting a stance towards the Bible which goes something like this – 'The Bible is partly the Word of God and partly the word of humans. In part it has authority and in part it has not.' This position leads to a view of the Bible that makes the Scriptures utterly useless and valueless. We are faced with a basic question: Who decides what is true? Who decides what is of value? The Bible declares for itself that *all* Scripture is God-breathed and that 'men spoke from God as they were carried along by the Holy Spirit' (2 Pet. 1:21). It is fully inspired by God but fully written by human agents. Christ Himself regarded the words of Isaiah and Moses as being the very words of God (Mark 7:5–13). Its amazingly fulfilled prophecies are just another indication of its divine inspiration.

When we examine the New Testament, we find that not only do writers such as John, Peter and Paul predict Christ's coming, but that Christ Himself taught us that one day He would return. 'I will come back,' He said (John 14:3). Amongst our Saviour's last words, in the book of Revelation, are these: 'Behold, I am coming soon' (22:7). Truly, as James Culross expresses it, 'If Christ were not to come, He would break His word.' Let us be quite clear about this. If Christ does not mean to return to this earth, if it is no part of His purpose personally to reappear in human history, if He really does not intend to come back to earth as corporeally as He once walked on earth, then He has perpetrated upon His followers a most cruel and heartless hoax. But Christ is coming back. In words that are crystal clear, He has told us so. Ian Macpherson, in his book *Dial the Future*, says,

> I expect to see Him [Christ] as literally as I have looked on David Ben Gurion. I await no disembodied wraith, no ectoplasmic emanation, no thin, impalpable apparition. I await the real Jesus, the One who ascended from Olivet and is to return to the same spot.[2]

Some Christians take the view that Christ returns each time a Christian dies, whilst others say that Christ returned in the power of the Spirit at Pentecost, but this was quite distinct and separate from His promised personal and physical return. Didn't the angels say, when Christ was taken up into heaven from Mount Olivet, 'This same Jesus... will come back in the same way you have seen him go into heaven'? How did He go? Visibly and physically. And that is how He will return.

Notes

---

2   1. Ian Macpherson, *Dial the Future* (Eastbourne: Prophetic Witness, 1975).

Discussion Starters

1. What is the purpose of Scripture?

_____
_____
_____
_____
_____

2. Why do we believe that all Scripture is inspired by God?

_____
_____
_____
_____
_____

3. In what sense is the Bible the word of humans and in what sense is it not?

_____
_____
_____
_____
_____

4. Why may people reject the concept that the whole Bible is divinely inspired?

_____
_____
_____
_____
_____

5. How did Christ validate the divine inspiration of the Bible?

_____
_____
_____
_____
_____

6. Why do we believe in the physical and personal return of Christ?

_____
_____
_____
_____
_____

7. What are the key differences between the first and second advents?

_____
_____
_____
_____
_____

8. Can you identify some fulfilled prophecies which indicate the divine inspiration of the Bible?

_____
_____
_____
_____
_____

Personal Application

Dr Martyn Lloyd-Jones, the outstanding Bible expositor, once said, 'Ultimately this question of the authority of the Scriptures is a matter of faith and not of argument... you may convince a man intellectually of what you're saying but still he may not of a necessity believe in and accept the authority of Scripture.'

Before Billy Graham went into the ministry, he wrestled with deep doubts about the reliability of the Bible. He said: 'But one day I decided to accept the Scriptures by faith. When I did this... it immediately became a flame in my hand. I found I could take a simple outline then put a number of Scripture quotations under each point, and God would use it mightily to cause men to make a full commitment to Christ.'

One of the greatest evidences of the Bible's authority is the fact that it does what it says it will do – convict, convert and change. Mary Warburton Booth sums up the feelings of all true believers when she cries:

> He is not a disappointment, He is coming by and by.
> In my heart I have the witness that His coming
>   draweth nigh.
> All the scoffers may despise me and no change around
>   me see,
> But He tells me He is coming and that's quite enough
>   for me.

Seeing Jesus in the Scriptures

Jesus treasured the Scriptures. He quoted them (Luke 4:1–12), read them (Luke 4:16–19), discussed them (Luke 10:25–37), taught from them (Luke 24:27), obeyed them (Luke 22:42) and ultimately fulfilled them (Luke 24:44). What an example for us!

Signs of the Times

Opening Exercise

Look at various Highway Code traffic signs individually or in your group. Can you correctly identify the meaning of each sign?

Bible Readings

- ▸ Ezekiel 36:22–24
- ▸ Ezekiel 37:1–14
- ▸ Matthew 24:1–44
- ▸ Luke 21:5–28
- ▸ 2 Thessalonians 2:1–4
- ▸ 2 Timothy 3:1–5

Opening Our Eyes

It cannot be denied that some of the signs that Christ and other biblical personalities give as pointing to the nearness of the second advent are characteristic of every age – wars, earthquakes, famines and so on. However, there are special signs which, by their very nature, can only be clearly understood and interpreted as the end actually draws near. It goes almost without saying that we must proceed very carefully on this matter as a good deal of damage has been done to the truth of the second advent by those who take the biblical signs out of context and push them too far. We must be equally diligent also that we do not miss what God is saying to us. The first sign is the global gospel. It has, of course, always been global in its commission: 'Go into all the world and preach the good news to all creation' (Mark 16:15). But it has never, until relatively recently, been fully global in its scope and outreach through such means as missionary societies and more latterly television, radio and the internet.

There is also the sign of multiplied lawlessness. Billy Graham, commenting on modern society, said, 'Compared to when I was a boy, we live life in reverse. The people are locked up in their homes at night and the criminals are outside on the loose!' Some historians are even saying that this present age, including the terrible bloodshed of two great world wars, is the most violent era in the history of the world. A third significant sign is the comparison with Noah's day. Jesus said, 'As it was in the days of Noah, so it will be at the coming of the Son of Man.' When the conditions before the Flood are repeated in history, the end is near, says Jesus. As it was... so it will be! What happened in Noah's day? There was an abnormal emphasis on sex, gluttony and rejection of God.

Our final sign is the establishing of the State of Israel and the return of the Jews to their promised homeland. Since the time of their destruction and dispersion among the Gentiles by the

Roman armies, the Jews have been scattered all across the face of the earth and have suffered acutely in all the countries where they fled for refuge. It is, indeed, a miracle that they have never been absorbed by the nations in which they have dwelt. All down the centuries, they have retained their distinctive, national characteristics. Humanly speaking, it seemed impossible that this despised and persecuted people could ever achieve national identity. However, now the impossible has become a fact. In May 1948 the modern State of Israel was established and in June 1967 Jerusalem became a Jewish city for the first time since 586 BC. The Bible, of course, predicted that one day this seemingly dead nation would spring to life. This is the whole point and purpose of the vision that Ezekiel had which we call 'the valley of dry bones'. God asks the prophet, 'Can these bones live?' In other words, how can a nation dispersed, ridiculed and driven to the ends of the earth be brought back together again? The only answer is through the power of God's eternal Spirit and we have seen the Jewish nation stand up before us as one of the greatest evidences in modern times of God's ability to fulfil His prophetic word.

Notes

_____
_____
_____
_____
_____
_____
_____
_____
_____
_____
_____
_____
_____
_____

Discussion Starters

1. Why should we be careful about signs such as earthquakes, wars and famines?

_____

_____

_____

_____

_____

2. Should we regard the extreme destructiveness of the Indonesian tsunami as a sign of the end times?

_____

_____

_____

_____

_____

3. Do you agree that today's lawless society is a sign of Christ's coming?

_____

_____

_____

_____

_____

4. How are the characteristics of Noah's day similar to our current age?

_____

_____

_____

_____

_____

5. Why have the Jewish people not been assimilated into the societies they emigrated to?

_____

_____

_____

_____

_____

6. How can the circumstances of Jewish people be regarded as a sign of Christ's return?

_____

_____

_____

_____

_____

7. Why did Christ explain the signs of the end of the age?

_____

_____

_____

_____

_____

8. How can we avoid obsession with these signs while faithfully watching for them?

_____

_____

_____

_____

_____

Personal Application

Christians are greatly divided on this subject. One school of thought claims that Jesus did not give His followers any particular sign but a baffling list of signs which are characteristic of the whole period between the resurrection of Jesus and His coming again. The advocates of this view also go on to say that the 'last days' spoken of in Scripture are not the few final years prior to Christ's return but the whole period from the resurrection to the second advent. Another school of thought, however (and one to which I subscribe), believes that whilst the Bible gives a list of general signs so that people in every generation might be 'kept on their toes', so to speak, there are at the same time, the special signs considered above. We greatly need the help of the Holy Spirit to avoid the excesses of obsession on the one hand and of 'putting our heads in the sand' on the other. After all, our Master told us to 'watch'.

We will consider 'living in the light of His coming' in more detail in Week Six, but for now we need to take care that we are not obsessed, deceived or shaken by world events and personalities. Rather, we should play our part in spreading the global gospel and faithfully representing Christ here on earth until He returns.

Seeing Jesus in the Scriptures

In passages such as Luke 13:1–5, we see that Jesus was always aware of events in His world and used them to warn people and call them into a relationship with God.

The Presence of Christ

Opening Exercise

What mementoes do people keep of family and friends that through distance (or death) they do not see often, and what benefits do they derive from those mementoes? Does anyone have a memento with them?

Bible Readings

- ▶ Matthew 18:20
- ▶ Matthew 28:18–20
- ▶ John 7:32–39
- ▶ John 14:16–26
- ▶ John 16:5–15
- ▶ Acts 2:1–4

Opening Our Eyes

We need to examine a question which often arises whenever the subject of the second coming is expounded. It is sometimes put like this: 'If Christ went back to heaven following His resurrection and is to return at the end of the age, does this mean that, at the present time, He is absent from the world and from His Church?' Far from it! Our Lord's final words as recorded by Matthew are: 'I am with you always, to the very end of the age' (28:20). No hint of any absence there! David Livingstone said of this verse, 'That is the promise of a perfect gentleman who never breaks his word.' Christ said in Matthew 18:20, 'For where two or three come together in my name, there am I with them.' Think about this verse with me for a moment. Jesus said 'I' will be among you – invisible but really there. What an exciting thought. Every great institution centres around some dominant personality. The United States finds its principle of cohesion in the presidency, the British Commonwealth of nations is integrated by its loyalty to the crown. However, there is an institution more wonderful than any nation or group of nations. And who is the personality that forms its organising focus? It is the risen Christ Himself. The Church here on earth finds its cohesion in the magnetism of an unseen yet ever-present Lord. Yet here is a paradox: Scripture affirms that Christ is both with us now but will also return. The answer to this paradox hinges on what happened at Pentecost.

Although the Holy Spirit was active in the world prior to Christ's coming, He was at a serious disadvantage because there was no perfect vehicle through whom He could express the purposes of God for the human race. The Holy Spirit would temporarily 'come upon' individuals to achieve God's purposes but could not permanently be 'in them'. Then Jesus came and, through His sinless life, substitutionary death and triumphant resurrection, established the model which God could use to develop Christlikeness in the sin-soiled human race. It is significant that the term 'Holy Spirit' is really a New Testament term. It is not found as such anywhere in the Old Testament. The content of

Jesus had not gone into it. 'Pentecost,' says Stephen Olford, 'could not be a reality until Calvary was a finality.' It is along a highway sprinkled with the precious blood of our Lord Jesus Christ that the Holy Spirit came to give Himself fully to the world. On the Day of Pentecost, the Holy Spirit, now having a perfect model to present to the world – the life and sacrificial character of Jesus – came to earth to apply the benefits of His life and death to the whole of the human race. The Holy Spirit, in a sense, has universalised Jesus; that is to say, He makes His life and presence known to millions of His followers across the face of the earth at one and the same time. Because we are physical beings, we long to see the face of our Master, but that joy must still await us. In the meantime, the Holy Spirit brings the life, the reality and the joy of Christ's presence into our hearts, so that although we know He is not physically present we experience His spiritual presence in a manner that is beyond expression.

Notes

_____
_____
_____
_____
_____
_____
_____
_____
_____
_____
_____
_____
_____
_____
_____
_____
_____

Discussion Starters

1. In what sense is Christ with us now?

2. Why was the Holy Spirit restricted in a way in Old Testament times?

3. What role does the Holy Spirit play in revealing Christ's presence to us?

4. How did Christ fix the content of the Holy Spirit in a way Samson did not?

5. In what ways does the Holy Spirit minister to us
and help us?

_____

_____

_____

_____

_____

6. What happened at Pentecost?

_____

_____

_____

_____

_____

7. If the Church finds its cohesion in Christ why are there so
many arguments between Christians?

_____

_____

_____

_____

_____

8. What is your personal experience of the Holy Spirit?

_____

_____

_____

_____

_____

Personal Application

Scripture invites us to be filled with the gentle, sacrificial, Christlike power of the Holy Spirit (Eph. 5:18). We can say quite categorically that if a person claims to be filled by the Holy Spirit but doesn't act like Jesus, then it isn't the Holy Spirit that inspires him but some other spirit.

Seeing Jesus in the Scriptures

As the power of the Holy Spirit was to be Christlike power, then it was necessary to see this power manifested through the whole gamut of Christ's life, from a carpenter's bench to the throne of the universe, from the denial, betrayal and crucifixion on the one hand to the triumph of the resurrection on the other. We had to see this power manifested on a cross, forgiving its enemies, and view it also as supreme modesty and humility as, when triumphing over those who crucified Him, our Lord refused to intimidate or overwhelm them by a demonstration of His deity. He was humble in every situation and yet almighty in that humility. The disciples who had walked with Jesus seemed to have the idea that Messianic power would be manifested in an overwhelming display that would compel obedience. But the reality was different! He overcame His enemies by loving them. Was this power final? Would it have the last word? The disciples had to see this power face everything, overcome everything, subdue everything and then go to the place of ultimate power – the throne of God. When the Spirit came to them at Pentecost, they knew then that this was ultimate power with ultimate character.

Life after Death

Opening Exercise

Briefly describe an event which has brought you great pleasure, such as a wedding, birth, award, holiday or sumptuous meal!

Bible Readings

- ▸ Psalm 16
- ▸ Luke 16:19–31
- ▸ Luke 23:32–43
- ▸ 2 Corinthians 5:1–9
- ▸ 1 Thessalonians 4:13–18

Opening Our Eyes

Before we look in detail at the manner of Christ's coming and what it will mean for the world, we have one more important question to examine – what happens to those who 'die in the Lord' prior to His coming? This must not be regarded as idle speculation, for the Bible has a good deal to say about what happens to Christians when they die. Dr W.E. Sangster in his book *These Things Abide* said, 'I have a section of my library given to guidebooks... It has long been my conviction that one must learn as much as possible about new lands before the journey begins.'[3]

The first thing the Bible teaches us about the state beyond death is that we shall enjoy the conscious presence of our Lord Jesus Christ. Some will disagree with me here as they believe that at death the spiritual part of a Christian lapses into a comatose condition from which they will emerge only when the last trumpet sounds. This view is sometimes referred to as 'soul sleep'. I do not believe that this is scripturally tenable. If Paul was not sure that he would consciously be in the presence of Christ immediately after death, why would he have said, 'I desire to depart, and be with Christ, which is better by far' (Phil. 1:23). He was already enjoying Christ's presence on earth. Would it be 'better by far' to leave that and go into a long state of unconscious hibernation?

I believe the Bible is quite clear on the fact that the moment a Christian dies, they go immediately into the presence of Christ. Here, their personality awaits the resurrection when their soul will be reunited with a new body. From passages such as Luke 16 we gather that after death we can still speak, think, hear, reason, see, remember and feel. What will it be like to be in our Master's presence awaiting the final day of resurrection? This blissful disembodied state will have many delights, but the one supreme

---

3   W.E. Sangster, *These Things Abide* (London: Hodder & Stoughton, 1939).

thing will be everlasting joy. How often heaven and joy are linked in the Bible. We read that 'there is rejoicing in the presence of the angels of God' (Luke 15:10). G. Campbell Morgan, commenting on this text, says, 'Notice it says "rejoicing in the presence of the angels of God". This indicates that in the heart of God Himself there is just no way that words can describe the bliss that throbs in His being when a sinner comes to know Him.' Again, we hear the Master say in the parable of the talents, 'Well done, good and faithful servant... Come and share your master's happiness!' There are eternal pleasures at His right hand (Psa. 16:11). I repeat, to be absent from the body means being present with the Lord and experiencing fullness of joy.

In a memorial service held in a church for a lady who had been a member there for many years, the minister pointed out that she had sat in the same seat at every service for as long as he could remember. That day, however, the seat was unoccupied – a mark of respect to her memory. The minister, taking advantage of that fact, pointed dramatically to the empty seat and cried, 'Absent!' Then pointing up to heaven, he cried, 'Present!' And that is Christian dying!

Notes

_____

_____

_____

_____

_____

_____

_____

_____

_____

_____

_____

_____

Discussion Starters

1. Why do people fear death?

2. What different views of death do people hold?

3. Why is the position of 'soul sleep' not tenable?

4. How can we be encouraged when fellow Christians die?

5. What does the story of Lazarus teach us about death?

6. How do you react to the concept of a God of joy and eternal pleasures?

_____
_____
_____
_____
_____

7. What joys do you think await us in heaven?

_____
_____
_____
_____
_____

8. Do you agree with the view that today's society talks too much about sex and too little about death?

_____
_____
_____
_____
_____

Personal Application

As believers, like Paul we need to develop a view of death that regards it as being a doorway into something that is much better – the immediate presence and joy of the Lord. Death is therefore something to be welcomed and not feared. Although we grieve our fellow believers, our mourning is tempered with a sense of celebration that they are now 'better by far' and we look forward to a wonderful reunion!

Seeing Jesus in the Scriptures

Jesus said to the thief on the cross, 'today you will be with me in paradise'. Later that day, Jesus' body was taken down from the cross, swathed in linen and placed on a ledge in Joseph of Arimathea's tomb, while the body of the malefactor was no doubt tossed into a pauper's grave. Yet the Saviour's prediction held good. The Redeemer and the repentant robber were together immediately after death, and being together would mean very little unless there was a conscious relationship. A person may be surrounded by a multitude of friends but if those friends are asleep, that person might as well be alone. As someone has pointed out, 'Those who sleep in Jesus are not asleep to Jesus.' They are consciously 'with Christ, which is better by far'. Some Christians say that it is pointless to speculate on whether a believer experiences after death the conscious presence of Christ, when we are certain that on the day of resurrection we shall see Him and be aware of Him. However, it is not speculation. Jesus' promise to the thief settles it – once and for all.

The Second Coming of Christ

Opening Exercise

Review our studies so far. What have you found particularly interesting and inspiring?

Bible Readings

- ▶ Matthew 24:3–36
- ▶ Acts 1:6–7
- ▶ 1 Thessalonians 4:13–18
- ▶ 2 Thessalonians 2:1–4
- ▶ Revelation 20:1–6

Opening Our Eyes

Although Christians accept the doctrine of Christ's second coming, there is much division on the subject of how and when His coming will take place. Three main views are held – all hinging on Revelation 20:6 which describes a reign of Christ and His people for 1,000 years (ie a millennium). One view, known as premillennialism, is that Christ will return prior to a 1,000-year reign. Another view, postmillennialism, is that the gospel will triumph throughout the world, producing a millennium of unparalleled joy, at the end of which Christ will return. Amillennialism holds that the description in Revelation 20 is symbolic and that it refers to the entire period of Christ's rule beginning with His ascension.

Most amillennialists see the promises of the Old Testament in relation to Israel as having their fulfilment in the Christian Church – the Israel of God. Amillennialists believe that a literal idea of a precise 1,000-year reign cannot be fitted into biblical eschatology[4] but is used as a symbol of the whole Church age. Amillennialists, for example, interpret the binding of Satan as described in Revelation 20:1–3 as having taken place when Christ came to this earth at the incarnation.

Postmillennialists (as the word suggests) believe that Christ will not return prior to a 1,000-year reign of bliss and blessedness but at the end of it. The Church, it is believed, acting as God's agent here on earth, will so influence the world by its life and witness that kingdom principles will triumph, and thus make the earth ready for the return of the King. A period of peace and prosperity is to precede rather than follow the return of Christ.

Premillennialism is a view which fails to answer all my questions but yet, more than the others, stimulates and satisfies me. First, it believes that prior to Christ's coming there will be a period of

---

4   The word 'eschatology' means 'the science or study of last things.

great apostasy – a falling away. Second, Jesus will come secretly for His saints and take both dead and living Christians to be with Himself – an event often referred to as 'the secret rapture' (see 1 Thess. 4:17). Once the Church has been raptured, there will be a 'reward tribunal' set up in the skies for believers, known as the *Bema* (Greek: reward seat), as explained in 2 Corinthians 5:10. Meanwhile a cataclysmic upheaval, known as the Great Tribulation, will take place down on earth. Fourth is the return of Christ to earth with His saints. This will take place at the end of the Great Tribulation, at which time Christ will descend to the Mount from which He ascended – Mount Olivet – whereupon He will supervise the great battle of Armageddon, and then usher in the 1,000-year reign of peace and prosperity known as the millennium. The final events in the timetable of premillennialism are as follows: Once Christ returns to Jerusalem, He will re-establish the Temple worship and, from there, with His saints, He will rule and reign over the earth for 1,000 years. After this 1,000-year reign has ended, Satan, who meantime had been bound, is loosed again and will be permitted to stir up rebellion against God. His period of activity will soon be restricted, however, whereupon he and his demons will be cast into the lake of fire. This will be followed by the resurrection and judgment of the wicked, after which comes the final eternal state.

Notes

Discussion Starters

1. What are the key features of the postmillennial view?

_____

_____

_____

_____

_____

_____

_____

_____

2. What are the key features of the amillennial view?

_____

_____

_____

_____

_____

_____

_____

3. What are the key features of the premillennial view?

_____

_____

_____

_____

_____

_____

_____

_____

4. Which view most appeals to you?

_____
_____
_____
_____
_____
_____
_____
_____

5. How could the different views affect the ministry of
the Church?

_____
_____
_____
_____
_____
_____
_____
_____

6. To what extent has the Church replaced Israel in the plan
and purposes of God?

_____
_____
_____
_____
_____
_____
_____
_____

Personal Application

Now that we have examined briefly the three main views concerning the second coming, are you still as confused as ever? If you are, don't worry. In the Christian Church at this moment such is the ministry of the Holy Spirit that He is drawing together men and women of different and divergent views and is making them one in spirit if not in understanding. I have many close and wonderful friends who take a different view from me on this subject, yet when we meet, we greet each other wholeheartedly because we know that although we have not yet achieved unanimity of belief, we can certainly enjoy the overriding unity of the Spirit. The whole point and purpose of eschatology is not simply to feed our minds but fire our hearts in expectation of His coming. The fact of His return is certain; it is merely the manner of His return that causes a difference of opinion. When we read our Bibles and alight on the truth of Christ's coming, we should, as someone has said, live as if He is coming today, and work as if He is not coming for another 1,000 years.

Seeing Jesus in the Scriptures

In the parable of the ten virgins in Matthew 25:1–13, Jesus is like the bridegroom. The virgins know he is coming, but they do not know the detail of his coming. Like them, we need to keep watch and be prepared for Jesus' return whenever and however that may happen.

Living in the Light of His Coming

Opening Exercise

Do you agree with the increasing use of speed cameras on our roads? How do they affect the behaviour of drivers?

How would you personally prepare, and what would you wear, if you were invited to a Buckingham Palace Garden Party?

Bible Readings

- ▶ Matthew 25:1–13
- ▶ Philippians 3:16–21
- ▶ 2 Peter 3
- ▶ 1 John 3:1–3

Opening Our Eyes

In the light of Christ's personal return to this world how then shall we live? The Scriptures imply that we should look for His coming with an eager and expectant heart. Are you eager to meet your Lord? C.S. Lewis said that some people find Christ's second coming a difficult doctrine for it cuts right across their aspirations and dreams. They want to make plans for a comfortable future and amass fortunes. But Jesus called them fools and said that when the end comes, 'who will get what you have prepared for yourself?' (Luke 12:20)

You see, it's one thing to hold the belief of the second coming in your head; it's another to let it control your heart. Is the truth of Christ's coming merely head knowledge or does it burn in the centre of your heart like a living flame?

In the last chapter of the Bible you will find two important phrases: 'I am coming soon' and 'Come, Lord Jesus'. We should so live that when Christ draws our attention to the phrase 'I am coming soon', our immediate response is one of joyful affirmation, 'Come, Lord Jesus.' There are some Christians who cannot wholeheartedly cry, 'Come, Lord Jesus' because they are still pursuing their own self-centred goals. For them, the return of Christ, if He came in this decade or generation, would mean the end of things they personally hold dear.

Secondly, we ought to live exemplary lives; 1 John 3:3 says, 'And every one who has this hope [resting] on Him cleanses [purifies] himself, just as He is pure – chaste, undefiled, guiltless' (Amplified). This verse corroborates that the whole point and purpose of prophecy is to tune our hearts to the fact that Christ is coming and that we should be ready for that all-important event. And how do we show ourselves to be ready? By living a pure and exemplary life.

Many years ago I visited a dear old saint in the Welsh valleys, 'What is the secret of your Christian character?' I asked him. He said, 'Ever since I was converted 60 years ago, I have tried to live before Him so that, should He come this day, I would not be ashamed at His coming.'

Thirdly, we ought to have an expressive and expendable faith. The Christian life is not merely a life of worship, it is also a life of witness. Our Lord's command is: 'Occupy till I come' (see Luke 19:13, KJV). Our Master expects us to share our faith with a world that does not know Him, and to make known in every way possible the reality of the Saviour's love, and the message that He is coming back again to this world. Sharing our faith, however, means more than just sharing a few facts about the Christian gospel – it means sharing ourselves. A friend of mine, Doug Barnett, made a statement which still rings in my ears. He said, 'We must stop trying to shout at people across a chasm, and start instead to build a relationship.' Isn't that the way many Christians go about sharing their faith? They talk to the unconverted in an aloof manner rather than build the bridge of a loving relationship which would, in turn, enhance the effectiveness of the message. We must remember that to share Jesus with the world means more than just the sharing of words – it means the sharing of ourselves.

Notes

Discussion Starters

1. How does the second coming affect your personal lifestyle?

_____

_____

_____

_____

_____

_____

2. Why may some Christians view the second coming with trepidation and others with eagerness?

_____

_____

_____

_____

_____

_____

3. In the light of the second coming, should Christians have no goals or ambitions?

_____

_____

_____

_____

_____

4. How can Christians ensure their lives are pure and holy, growing in love and faith?

_____

_____

_____

_____

_____

_____

5. How can the second coming inspire us to greater levels of evangelism?

_____

_____

_____

_____

_____

_____

6. Do you have any concerns about sharing your faith?

_____

_____

_____

_____

_____

_____

7. How can we share ourselves as well as our message?

_____

_____

_____

_____

_____

_____

Personal Application

The truth of the second coming should impact us in three ways: an expectant heart, a godly lifestyle and a passionate desire to share our life and faith with others. The age through which we are passing is one of supreme indifference to the claims of Christ. What do you do when people just don't care? Keep on caring – Jesus did. Love does not change, no matter the attitude of the other person. To allow other people and circumstances to determine your conduct and attitudes is to become a mere reflection, the sum total of the attitudes of others. I am told that in the Andes mountains when the pack goats meet each other on a rocky ledge where it is difficult to pass, one will kneel and let the other pass over him, to the safety of both. In order to share your faith effectively perhaps you will have to kneel to let someone walk over you. If you are to be a bridge between someone's indifference and their awakening, you will be walked on. It will require more than words. It will require deeds like sharing people's concerns, joys, problems and sufferings. And that's costly. To try and share our faith merely by words without being willing to win people's trust and earn the right to their attention, is not the pattern set by our Master.

Seeing Jesus in the Scriptures

Jesus was consumed with zeal to fulfil God's plan (John 2:17). He lived a pure life. He not only preached to the poor but served, fed and healed them.

A Bride for God's Son

Opening Exercise

Ask members of the group to share photographs from joyous occasions, such as family weddings. What are their memories of such a special day?

Bible Readings

- ▸ Genesis 2:19–25
- ▸ Ephesians 1:3–14
- ▸ Ephesians 5:25–32
- ▸ 1 Peter 1:18–21
- ▸ Revelation 13:8
- ▸ Revelation 19:5–9

Opening Our Eyes

It is time to gain a more eternal perspective. In my view, the Bible shows that behind the creation, God had in mind the completion of a supreme and breathtaking achievement – the selection of a bride for His Son. That purpose can be seen also in the creation of the first man and woman. After creating Adam from the dust of the earth, God put him into a deep sleep and took from his side a rib, out of which He formed the woman. Why didn't God make Eve out of the dust of the ground in the same way that He made Adam? Why the necessity to create her from one of his ribs? I believe that God wanted to lay deep in human consciousness the concept that humanity owes its existence to a man being introduced into the world, a bride being constructed from out of his side and then being joined to him again by God so that the two became one. There in that act of human creation, you have a perfect picture of what God designed for His Son. On the cross, God took from the body of the Lord Jesus Christ the element of blood, and in that blood He washes all those who in simple faith surrender to Him. At the cross, a new humanity is created – a company of blood-washed people who will one day be married to Christ in eternity.

God had a Lamb before He had a Man. When God laid down the broad beams of creation in the distant ages of the past, He made the cross an integral part of the universe. Christian teachers have always insisted that Christ was once offered for sins and that Calvary is a fact of recorded time. With this there can be no disagreement, but we must also see that before there was a cross raised on Calvary, there was a cross built into the universe from the very foundation of the world. God foreknew that His plan to provide a perfect bride for His perfect Son could be thwarted by humanity's sin and therefore prepared a perfect sacrifice and perfect redemption. In eternity past before the creation of the world, we were chosen in Him and our sacrificial Lamb was chosen for us. Adam's sin did not surprise God for He had already planned a way to overcome it!

When precisely this royal wedding between Christ and the Church will take place depends once again on one's views of the second coming. Some believe it will happen between the rapture and return of Christ with His saints to the earth. Others believe it will be ushered in with the millennium. They see the nuptial celebrations as extending over 1,000 years. We may not be able to say with absolute accuracy when it will take place but we can say with certainty that it will take place. And that is what is all-important. Paul says of this marriage union between Christ and His Church: 'the two will become one... This is a profound mystery – but I am talking about Christ and the church.' Reflect on that for a moment. What is the 'profound mystery'? When Christ comes to take us to be with Himself, He is not going to transform us into angelic beings – He is going to make us one with Himself. We shall be made like Him – a perfect partner for the perfect Bridegroom.

Notes

_____
_____
_____
_____
_____
_____
_____
_____
_____
_____
_____
_____
_____
_____
_____
_____
_____
_____

Discussion Starters

1. Why was Eve created from Adam's rib and not from dust like him?

_____

_____

_____

_____

_____

2. In what way are Adam and Eve like Christ and the Church?

_____

_____

_____

_____

_____

3. Why do we know that sin did not take God by surprise?

_____

_____

_____

_____

_____

4. What did God do before the creation?

_____

_____

_____

_____

_____

5. Why are we superior to angels?

_____

_____

_____

_____

_____

6. What does God think about you?

_____

_____

_____

_____

_____

7. What does Christ think about you?

_____

_____

_____

_____

_____

8. What has particularly impacted you in our studies of the second coming?

_____

_____

_____

_____

_____

Personal Application

I know of no better way of ending our studies on the subject of the second coming than by gazing out into eternity. What faces us in those endless ages where time will be no more? Paul in 1 Corinthians 15:24 says, 'Then the end will come'. The end of what? The end of sin's reign, the end of injustice, the end of everything inimical to the righteousness of God. However, in one sense the end is but the beginning. It will be the beginning of an existence in which sin and Satan will have no part and where bliss and blessedness will reign supreme. Some people are put off by the biblical pictures of heaven and eternity which speak of palms, white robes, crowns and harps. Don't allow yourself to be adversely affected by this, for such descriptions can only take us to the edge of things – beyond lies a state that no language can adequately convey. There is a beautiful story about a small blind girl whose sight was restored by a brilliant surgeon. When the bandages were removed, the girl exclaimed, 'Oh, Mummy, why didn't you tell me it was as lovely as this.' Brushing away her tears, the mother replied, 'My darling, I did my best to tell you but there were just not enough words to describe it. You had to see it for yourself.' Similarly, the delights and wonders of eternity are ultimately indescribable.

Seeing Jesus in the Scriptures

Jesus is our Lord, Saviour, Teacher, Friend, Brother, Joint Heir, but ultimately, our beloved and loving Bridegroom.

Leader's Notes

WEEK ONE: Basis of Belief in the Second Coming

Exercise

By and large many people now regard the Bible as just one of a number of religious books. It may contain some wisdom from a bygone era but is generally no longer relevant in today's hi-tech multicultural society. Our first task therefore is to validate the importance and divine inspiration of the Bible, for it is in the Bible that we read of the second coming. If the Bible is not authoritative, then the second coming may be a figment of the writers' imaginations.

Bible Readings

References such as Exodus 20:1, Jeremiah 48:1 and Malachi 1:1 clearly show that the Bible contains God's words and not just human poetry, prediction or wisdom.

Aim of the Session

The Old Testament refers to two advents – Christ coming as a baby to Bethlehem and, at some point in the future, His coming in triumph to judge the wicked, redeem the righteous and purge the earth of all evil. All the Old Testament references relating to Christ's coming have to be carefully examined to see whether they refer to His first or second advent. Many of the teachers in ancient Israel failed to differentiate between the two advents, and this is why, when Christ arrived in Bethlehem 2,000 years ago, He was largely unexpected. Isaiah 53:1–9 and Daniel 7:13–14 show quite clearly the difference between the two advents. First, He would come as a suffering servant and then as a triumphant King. Why, we ask ourselves, did so many miss this truth? Perhaps it was because they leaned too much on their own abilities and were only prepared to accept from the Scriptures what they themselves wanted and could understand.

One of the strongest objective arguments for the validity of Scripture comes from fulfilled Bible prophecy. Peter Stoner, a brilliant scientist and a Christian, has utilised what is called the 'principle of probability' in relation to Bible prophecy[5]. This principle holds that if the chance of one thing happening is one in M and the chance of another thing happening is one in N, the chance that they both shall happen is one in MxN. This equation is used in fixing insurance rates. Stoner asked 600 of his students to apply the principle of probability to the prophecy of the destruction of Tyre as found in Ezekiel 26:3–16. In this prophecy seven definite events are predicted.

(1) Nebuchadnezzar would take the city. (2) Other nations would help. (3) Tyre would be flattened like the top of a rock. (4) The city would become a place where fishermen would spread their nets. (5) Tyre's stones and timbers would be laid in the sea. (6) Other cities would fear because of Tyre's fall. (7) The old city of Tyre would not be rebuilt. Using the principle of probability, the students calculated that the chances of all seven events occurring as described was one in 400 million. Yet all seven did occur. Biblical prophecy declares the events of the future with an accuracy which is beyond the capability of human wisdom or anticipation. Despite astronomical odds, hundreds of biblical prophecies have come true, and this, apart from anything

5   Peter Stoner, *Science Speaks* (Moody Press, 1963).

else, is an impressive tribute to the authority and reliability of the Scriptures. Other notable examples would be prophecies fulfilled by Christ such as His place of birth, slaughter of the innocents, return from Egypt, ministry, manner of death and resurrection. Also, the return of the Jews to Israel after nearly 2,000 years.

Interestingly, Peter regarded Paul's writings as divinely inspired Scripture (2 Pet. 3:15–16) and Paul in 1 Timothy 5:18 equally regarded both Deuteronomy 25:4 and Luke 10:7 as 'Scripture'.

WEEK TWO: Signs of the Times

Exercise
A simple but hopefully amusing way to encourage people to think about signs and their meanings. Give the winner a small prize such as a bar of chocolate!

Bible Readings
It may also be helpful to read Genesis 6:1–8 which explains the conditions in Noah's day.

Aim of the Session
Noah's day was a period of great gluttony. The men and women of his day were interested solely in indulging their physical appetites, and had no thought for deeper or more important things. Here in the West, people have become gluttons; even our dogs are better fed than millions of people in the developing world! Another feature of Noah's day was a falling away from the faith. In Jude 11 the Bible talks about those who have gone the way of Cain. Cain lived before Noah. He led the violence and lawlessness that eventually caused God to send the Flood. Cain believed in God. He had heard the Almighty speak to him from heaven. His error was that he decided to ignore God's requirement for a blood sacrifice and instead attempted to substitute a humanistic type of religion. Isn't this what is taking place all around us today? Multitudes who believe in God are,

nevertheless, going the way of Cain. They ignore God's plan of salvation – the cross – and substitute it for a religion of good works. Another aspect of this lawlessness is that according to 2 Thessalonians 2:1–4, it seems that prior to 'the day of the Lord', an evil and wicked personality called 'the man of lawlessness' will arise and have world influence. His skill at diplomacy and his ability to handle a crisis will be so effective that many nations will be eager to co-operate with him, if only for the security of their own people and the stability of their own economy. He will oppose anything that has to do with the true God and will seek to exalt himself to a position higher than God. However, we must beware idle speculation as to his identity and notice that he is 'doomed to destruction'.

So important is the sign of the re-emergence of the nation of Israel that it is worth considering it more fully. In Luke 21:24, Jesus talks about 'the times of the Gentiles' being fulfilled. Some Bible scholars think that the times of the Gentiles began in 586 BC when Nebuchadnezzar sacked the city, destroyed the Temple and deported some of the Jews to Babylon (2 Kings 25:8–11). From that time to this present generation, Jerusalem has been under the domination of Gentile forces – 'the times of the Gentiles'. However, on 7 June 1967, Israeli troops advanced in a pincer movement on the old city of Jerusalem and took over control. Hardbitten soldiers wept as their chaplain-general blew the blast of Jubilee on his shofar or ram's horn. Israeli General Moshe Dayan placed a piece of paper, containing a written prayer, in one of the cracks in the Western Wall, remarking, 'We have reached the holiest of our holy places, never to go back.' Whether that is true remains to be seen, but one can't help but stand in utter amazement before the events that have transpired in the last 60 years and marvel at the accuracy of God's Word.

In the light of our Saviour's words, what I have described is immensely significant; when this happens, He says, 'they will see the Son of Man'. I ask myself, along with thousands of other

Christians as we witness the miracle of Israel: How close must Christ's coming be?

WEEK THREE: The Presence of Christ

Exercise

No illustrations are perfect but it is interesting the comfort and pleasant feelings we experience when we consider mementoes such as photographs, letters, keepsakes and gifts. At such times we almost sense the person's presence with us. The Holy Spirit is no memento but a real Person.

Bible Reading

The readings reveal Christ's promise of His presence and the Holy Spirit for every believer.

Aim of the Session

It is important for us to realise that although Christ is not physically present with us in this age, He is nevertheless spiritually present to minister His grace, comfort and love to us through the Holy Spirit. Scripture says quite clearly in John 7:39 that the Holy Spirit could not be given until Jesus had been glorified. Yet when we open the Old Testament, we find evidence of the Holy Spirit being at work in a variety of ways. He was active, for example, in the creation of the universe: 'and the Spirit of God was hovering over the the waters' (Gen. 1:2). He was active, too, in the life of Bezaleel who played a major part in the construction of the ancient Tabernacle: 'I have filled him with the Spirit of God' (Exod. 31:3). He was active again in the life of Samson, of whom the Bible says, 'the Spirit of the LORD began to stir him' (Judg. 13:25). Over and over again in the Old Testament, we see evidence of the Holy Spirit at work. What then does Scripture mean when it says that the Spirit could not be given until after Jesus' glorification? Although the Spirit was at work in the world prior to the coming of Christ, He was not fully active because there was no perfect vehicle through whom

He could manifest Himself. This is why the Spirit's intervention in human affairs in Old Testament times was always special, partial and occasional. The Holy Spirit, having achieved a particular purpose, returned to heaven, waiting, as did the dove in Noah's time, for a point and a place on which He could not only rest but remain. It was necessary for Jesus to complete His mission of redemption before the Holy Spirit could reveal Himself fully to the world.

'God,' said one writer, 'could not give the Spirit fully to men until Jesus had fixed the content of the Spirit.' Why was it necessary for Jesus to 'fix the content' of the Spirit? Because by viewing the ministry of the Holy Spirit in the Old Testament alone, we could arrive at wrong conclusions about Him. Take this verse, for example, 'The spirit of the Eternal inspired him [Samson] mightily; he went down to Ashkelon, where he killed thirty of the citizens, [and] plundered them' (Judg. 14:19, Moffatt). There are, of course, good reasons why God acted in this way in Old Testament times. However, the Old Testament must not be considered to be the full and final declaration of God's purposes and revelation – it was a point in a line leading forward to the full and final revelation as caught up and expressed through Jesus.

It is important that we see the Holy Spirit is not a mere influence – He is a Person. Jesus refers to the Holy Spirit as 'He' and so by using the personal pronoun in John 16:7–14, indicates that the Spirit is a Person with the qualities of will, intelligence, emotion etc. Make no mistake about it, when we come in contact with the Holy Spirit, we come in contact with a Person who is co-equal with God in rank, status and power.

WEEK FOUR: Life after Death

Exercise

One of the key aspects of life after death is joy – and that joy will be greater than anything we have known on earth!

Bible Readings

Note the readings are meant to encourage us, not depress us!

Aim of the Session

We need to understand that for a believer death is not annihilation or 'soul sleep' but a passing from this earthly life into a life of joy in the immediate presence of the Lord. Herbert Lockyer observes:

> Care must be taken to show that sleep, when applied to death, refers only to the body, not to the soul. The dust sleeps in the earth awaiting resurrection, but the soul of the Christian is as conscious the hour after death as the hour before it.

In order to gain some perspective to this subject of death, let us examine the various views which people hold on this matter. Some believe that death is extinction – life is over when this life is over. Humans are a chemical combination and life is no more than a flame which comes from a chemical combination – when the flame dies, we die. Some believe in reincarnation. They say that since this life is too short and too indeterminate to work out our final destiny, we will come back again – be reborn on a higher or lower scale of existence according to our deeds. The Bible does not support either view. The human race does not need reincarnation but regeneration in this incarnation. Universalism propounds that everybody will be finally saved. Those who hold this doctrine believe that one day the love of God will overwhelm all human wilfulness and that everyone will be given a place in Christ's universal kingdom. This doctrine fails to take into account that humanity is free and can decide for or against the love of God. Close to this theory runs the doctrine of a 'second chance'. Will there be another chance to accept Jesus Christ as Lord and Saviour in the next life? I do not believe so. However, while I do not believe in a second chance, I do believe in an adequate chance. Infants, those with learning disabilities, those dying before reaching the age of responsibility and those who, for various reasons, have not had an adequate chance, I safely leave in the hands of God knowing, as Genesis 18:25 says, 'Will not the Judge of all the earth do right?' I believe that God will provide for them in harmony with His eternal principles. However, this does not mean that we can preach the gospel of a second chance in another life. We can only preach the gospel of an adequate chance in this life. The only safe thing is to decide now.

What happens to the person who wilfully spurns the offer of life in Christ and dies in an unrepentant state? His soul goes to a place called Hades (hell) where he remains until the final judgment. I am conscious of the fact that hell is not a very pleasant subject to talk about, or even to write about. It is unpopular, controversial and greatly misunderstood. However, the Bible is quite clear on the issue, and we must not shrink from facing up to what the Scriptures teach concerning hell. God doesn't send anyone to hell. The unrepentant soul sends itself, with God blocking the way at every step and reminding it by every means possible – the moral universe, the orderly creation and the message of the gospel – that to go against the will of the Creator is to consign oneself to banishment from His presence.

WEEK FIVE: The Second Coming of Christ

Exercise
It would be beneficial to review our past studies to bring clarity prior to this session which contains conflicting views on the exact nature of Christ's return.

Bible Readings
It may be important to highlight that although the central message of Jesus' return is clear, God has deliberately kept some details to Himself!

Aim of the Session
We should seek to understand the three main views of Christ's return. A proof text of the amillennialists is Matthew 12:28. 'But if it is by the Spirit of God that I drive out the demons, then the kingdom of God has come upon you [before you expected it]' (Amplified). Amillennialists believe that the first resurrection and the reign of the saints with Christ is not something that is to take place in the future but that it has taken place in the past. They see the first resurrection as either the new life a person receives when he comes to Christ (Eph. 2:5) or the victory of the martyred saints in heaven. We are in the millennium now, say the amillennialists, and although there are different shades of interpretation within this particular school, most believe that the millennium is symbolic and not a literal 1,000-year reign.

One postmillenialist, Loraine Boettner, sees the task of the Church as not simply to evangelise the world but to Christianise it. He claims that by the efforts of the Church and its evangelistic activities, society will be changed and the glory of the Lord will cover the earth. Postmillennialists also view the language of the book of Revelation as symbolical of God's working through history. Beyond its confusing symbols and complicated patterns, there is one basic message – God's ability to turn all things to good, and bring about on earth the triumph of the kingdom of God. Prophecies relating to the Jewish nation are applied to the Church, seeing the Church as the new Israel – the 'Israel of God' (Gal. 6:16). Postmillennialists see in Ezekiel's valley of dry bones something other than that Israel will one day be gathered together as a nation. They see rather a picture of the Christian Church being brought together bone by bone (united by the Spirit), clothed with living flesh (baptised afresh with the gifts of God), welded together into a mighty army that will go out into the world and make a mighty impact for God.

The word 'rapture', like the term 'second coming', is not a biblical word. It is derived from the Latin Vulgate where it transliterates the term 'caught up' in 1 Thessalonians 4:17. The closest English equivalent to the Greek used by Paul is to 'snatch' or 'grab', implying the swiftest possible seizure. At some time in the future, say the premillennialists, Christ will come secretly and silently to catch away, 'rapture', His saints. This is not the same event as His coming to earth. It will take place in the air prior to His coming to earth when the saints, whether dead or alive, will rise into a new and radiant life. They will be changed, according to Scripture, 'in a flash, in the twinkling of an eye' (1 Cor. 15:51–52). Some believe that the Church will entirely escape the Great Tribulation; others think she will escape only a part of it. It is believed that the period of the Great Tribulation will last about seven years. This is based on the missing heptad (a series or group of seven) of Daniel's seventy weeks (Dan. 9:24–27), sixty-nine of which were accomplished before the cutting off of the Messiah (Christ's crucifixion) and one of which awaits fulfilment.

WEEK SIX: Living in the Light of His Coming

Exercise

Behaviour and personal appearance tend to alter when we feel ourselves under scrutiny or when we are due to meet special people.

Bible Readings

You could also refer to Matthew 6:25–34, showing the natural process of growth and the futility of worrying about earthly concerns.

Aim of the Session

Our aim is to come to a realisation that the truth of Christ's second coming should affect our lifestyles. Belief should impact behaviour. It is one thing to believe in Christ's second coming but it is entirely another thing to actually live in the light of it. What are our priorities? Are they centred in gold or in God? Do we look forward to the coming of Christ with true Christian joy? Or does the prospect displease us because if He came soon it would terminate some of our plans and ambitions? Bible scholars of all persuasions have pointed out that the subject of the second coming does not drop into a simple and straightforward mould as do other Bible doctrines like the atonement, justification by faith, the Holy Spirit and so on. They believe that God has arranged it this way on purpose so that we will not spend too much time focusing on dates, periods and signs, and so miss the whole point of the biblical references to the second coming. What is the purpose of such references? It is to tune our hearts and modify our lifestyles so that we are ready for that all-important event. What if those of the premillennial persuasion discover that the return of the Jews to their promised homeland is just coincidental after all, and that events in the Middle East come to a safe and happy conclusion? Or what if the postmillennialists discover that armies from the north move towards Jerusalem in line with the prophecies in Ezekiel, and events drop into place as the premillennialists believe? We must not tie ourselves too rigidly to any view but, like the early Christians, look not so much for signs but for the Lord Himself. Practically every book of the New Testament bears witness to this fact – they lived as if Christ would come at any moment. And so must we!

Does this mean that we must start every day with a period of intense self-examination and ask ourselves: Am I pure enough, holy enough, good enough to meet Christ if He were to come today? No! Some Christians are so introspective, so self-preoccupied, that they miss the sheer joy of sharing their lives hour by hour, day by day with Jesus. The very first law of life is receptivity. The first act of a child is to receive. Instinctively, as soon as it is born, the child turns to its mother's breast – to receive. The first law of life – receptivity – begins there and goes through the whole of life. We can expend only what we receive and no more. Jesus said, 'See how the lilies of the field grow.' How do they grow? By striving, getting into an agony of desire to grow, by frantic effort? No, the lilies grow by receptivity. They take in from the soil and sun and they give back in beauty. They grow effortlessly without strain and without drain. So Jesus points us to the lilies and asks us to grow by receptivity. The nervous, overactive Christian, struggling to achieve more purity and holiness, is not what God wants or expects. Simply focus on Christ, rejoice in the fact that He loves you – and grow as the lilies grow, by the law of the Great Intake.

WEEK SEVEN: A Bride for God's Son

Exercise

You may need to be sensitive if there are people who have been widowed, who are separated, unmarried and childless etc.

Bible Readings

Take time to read and especially highlight the eternal truths of the 'profound mystery' of these passages. Also, the Song of Songs is often seen as a picture of Christ's love for His Church.

Aim of the Session

Many think that the cross was God's rescue attempt after He was surprised by humankind's sin and that we are merely 'saved sinners'; God chose us because of Jesus' sacrifice. In fact, a careful study of the New Testament reveals that we were chosen before creation and were chosen not just to be God's slaves or even His sons but to be part of the perfect bride for His Son. This was His ultimate intention even before the worlds were formed. There is therefore a romantic purpose that lies at the heart of the universe. We are not a nuisance to God, but precious to Him.

The self-sacrifice that expressed itself through the cross at Calvary is reflected in all parts of God's creation. The seed dies that the plant may live. The plant dies that the soil might be enriched. White blood cells die that other parts of the body might be healthy. Right through God's creation runs this message – out of death flows life. The facts of history point towards the truth that at the heart of creation there is a cross. At the cross, Satan made the biggest blunder of his career for, by bringing about the death of Christ, he played right into the hands of God. When Adam sinned in the beginning, being the representative of the human race that was to follow, he handed over the title deeds of humanity, so to speak, to the devil. From that moment until Christ's death on Calvary, the human race was in debt to Satan. Christ, being the representative of a new order of humanity, was able by His death to redeem men and women and open up to them the potential of transferring their allegiance from Satan to God. At the cross, therefore, Satan lost his legal rights to the title deeds of humanity and now all those who by an act of free will commit themselves to Jesus Christ, are delivered from the bondage of sin and Satan, and are made heirs of God and joint heirs with Christ. When Satan and his minions saw what happened to Christ on the cross, no doubt they gleefully cried: 'We did it!' But as God looked down and saw the redemption of the race being accomplished by the death of His only Son, He would have said, 'I did it.' Whose message does the cross now beam out to the whole universe? Satan's or God's?

I believe that when God made Adam in the beginning, He made him with a complex nature; he contained, in a perfectly balanced way, a masculine and feminine nature. My basis for believing this is Genesis 5:2. 'Male and female created he them; and blessed them, and called their name [plural] Adam [singular]' (KJV). Notice what it says, 'He called their name Adam.' I take this to mean that God put the woman in the man, then later took her out of the man and then joined her yet again to him, to become bone of his bone and flesh of his flesh. Similarly, the Church, the bride of Christ, was actually in Christ in eternity, taken out of Him in time, and will be joined together again with Him in the eternity that is to come.

Daily Guide

This Daily Guide is designed to help you to engage with the material in the Study Guide between the sessions. More copies of this daily guide are available to download for free from **wvly.org/c2ccv.**

Day 1	Complete Week 1 in the Study Guide
Day 2	Read 2 Timothy 3:10-17, and memorise verses 16,17
Day 3	Prayer for the day: help me increase my interest in your Word
Day 4	Action: Spend 15 minutes reading the Bible and ask God to highlight a verse or verses to you
Day 5	Read 2 Peter 1:16-21
Day 6	Prayer for the day: Thank you God for revealing your will and ways to me through your Word
Day 7	Action: Look for opportunities to talk to someone about the value of the Bible today
Day 8	Complete Week 2 in the Study Guide
Day 9	Read Matthew 24:1-44
Day 10	Prayer for the day: Thank you that the Gospel is reaching more and more people worldwide through radio, satellite TV and the Internet. Bless those who provide the technology to make it happen

Day 11   Action: Think of a country where you know little about the church within it and use google to see what you can find and pray for that church

Day 12   Read 2 Thessalonians 2:1-4

Day 13   Prayer for the day: Thank you God that you are at work in all nations in the world and will bring people of every tribe and tongue and nation to know you

Day 14   Action: Look for opportunities to talk to someone about what they think about the future for the world

Day 15   Complete Week 3 in the Study Guide

Day 16   Read Matthew 28:19-20

Day 17   Prayer for the day: Lord help me to be conscious of your presence today

Day 18   Action: Set a timer on your phone for each hour and when it buzzes thank God for his presence with you

Day 19   Read John 14:16-26

Day 20   Prayer for the day: Today help me to see things as you see them, as your Spirit gives me revelation

Day 21   Action: Spend a minute: breathe in (welcome the Holy Spirit's filling) breathe out (expel anything that disturbs your peace)

Day 22   Complete Week 4 in the Study Guide

Day 23   Read Psalm 16

Day 24   Prayer for the day: I choose today to put you in all the situations that I will face, and know that I have nothing to fear

Day 25   Action: Look for an opportunity to gently talk with someone about what they think will happen to them after death

Day 26   Read 2 Corinthians 5:1-9

Day 27   Prayer for the day: Thank you for my body, the bits I like and the bits I am not keen on. Give me grace as it ages and thanks for the refit I will have in the life to come.

Day 28   Action: Pray for anyone you know who is recently bereaved and if prompted drop them a note, email or text to tell them you were thinking of them

Day 29 Complete Week 5 in the Study Guide

Day 30 Read Revelation 20:1-6

Day 31 Prayer for the day: Help me to live today with the awareness that Jesus could return at any time

Day 32 Action: Look for charts online that suggest the order of the Second Coming and decide which you think works best

Day 33 Read 1 Thessalonians 4:13-18

Day 34 Prayer for the day: Thank you that one day all be well and so we can have hope in you

Day 35 Action: Share your sense of hope with someone you know

Day 36 Complete Week 6 in the Study Guide

Day 37 Read Philippians 3:16-21

Day 38 Prayer for the day: God, I depend on you today to shine through me to those I meet

Day 39 Action: Do anything which God has told you to do which you haven't yet done

Day 40 Read 1 John 3:1-3

Day 41 Prayer for the day: Thank you that you are intending to see me grow into the likeness of Jesus. I trust you today to lead me on

Day 42 Action: Talk to someone about what you have been studying in this course and why it has been helpful

Day 43 Complete Week 7 in the Study Guide

The Cover to Cover Bible Study Series

CHARACTERS

Abraham
Adventures of faith
ISBN: 978-1-78259-089-7

Barnabas
Son of encouragement
ISBN: 978-1-85345-911-5

David
A man after God's own heart
ISBN: 978-1-78259-444-4

Elijah
A man and his God
ISBN: 978-1-85345-575-9

Elisha
A lesson in faithfulness
ISBN: 978-1-78259-494-9

Jacob
Taking hold of God's blessing
ISBN: 978-1-78259-685-1

Joseph
The power of forgiveness and reconciliation
ISBN: 978-1-85345-252-9

Mary
The mother of Jesus
ISBN: 978-1-78259-402-4

Moses
Face to face with God
ISBN: 978-1-85345-336-6

THEMES

Bible Genres
Hearing what the Bible really says
ISBN: 978-1-85345-987-0

Covenants
God's promises and their relevance today
ISBN: 978-1-85345-255-0

The Creed
Belief in action
ISBN: 978-1-78259-202-0

The Divine Blueprint
God's extraordinary power in ordinary lives
ISBN: 978-1-85345-292-5

Fruit of the Spirit
Growing more like Jesus
ISBN: 978-1-85345-375-5

God's Rescue Plan
Finding God's fingerprints on human history
ISBN: 978-1-85345-294-9

Great Prayers of the Bible
Applying them to our lives today
ISBN: 978-1-85345-253-6

The Holy Spirit
Understanding and experiencing Him
ISBN: 978-1-85345-254-3

The Image of God
His attributes and character
ISBN: 978-1-85345-228-4

Names of God
Exploring the depths of God's character
ISBN: 978-1-85345-680-0

NEW: Revival
Seeking and encountering abundant life
ISBN: 978-1-78951-441-4

Rivers of Justice
Responding to God's call to righteousness today
ISBN: 978-1-85345-339-7

The Second Coming
Living in the light of Jesus' return
ISBN: 978-1-85345-422-6

The Uniqueness of our Faith
What makes Christianity distinctive?
ISBN: 978-1-85345-232-1

NEW: Violence against Women
Discovering El Roi, The God Who Sees
ISBN: 978-1-78951-445-2

NEW TESTAMENT

NEW: Matthew
Your Kingdom Come
ISBN: 978-1-78951-450-6

Mark
Life as it is meant to be lived
ISBN: 978-1-85345-233-8

Luke
A prescription for living
ISBN: 978-1-78259-270-9

John's Gospel
Exploring the seven miraculous signs
ISBN: 978-1-85345-295-6

Acts 1–12
Church on the move
ISBN: 978-1-85345-574-2

Acts 13–28
To the ends of the earth
ISBN: 978-1-85345-592-6

For current prices or to order, visit **waverleyabbeytrust.org/publishing**